MENTAL HEALTH ISSUES

A doctor's Reflection

On Mental Health Issues;

Causes, Symptoms &

Treatments.

Dr. Fred Haturo

DEDICATION

To everyone who has faced the shadows of their mind,

This book is dedicated to your strength and resilience.

Your journey is important, and your story matters.

We are in this together. Always seek help.

TABLE OF CONTENTS

Dedication

Introduction

BOOK ONE: **ANXIETY DISORDER**..........1

BOOK TWO: **DEPRESSION (DEPRESSIVE DISORDER)**....................23

BOOK THREE: **BIPOLAR DISORDER**.......36

BOOK FOUR: **POST-TRAUMATIC STRESS DISORDER(PTSD)**...................47

BOOK FIVE: **SCHIZOPHENIA**.................67

BOOK SIX: **EATING DISORDER**.............79

CONCLUSION:...................89

WHO RESPONSE:.............................92

INTRODUCTION

A broad spectrum of mental health illnesses that impact your mood, thoughts, and behavior are collectively referred to as mental illness, often known as mental health disorders. Generally, there are four types of mental health disorders;

Mood disorders (such as depression or bipolar disorder), Anxiety disorders. Personality disorders, and Psychotic disorders (such as schizophrenia). Others are eating disorders which are prevalent in women. Hormonal changes related to menstrual cycles, pregnancy, and menopause can also impact mental health.

Many people also experience stigma, discrimination and violations of human rights. A clinically significant disruption in an individual's behavior, emotion regulation, or thought processes is indicative of a mental disease. Usually, it is linked to distress or impairment in critical domains of functioning. There are numerous varieties of mental illnesses. Mental health issues are another name for mental disorders. The latter is a more general phrase that encompasses psychosocial disabilities, mental disorders, and (other) mental states linked to substantial distress, functional impairment, or self-harm risk.

In 2019, 970 million individuals worldwide, or 1 in every 8 persons, suffered from a mental illness. Anxiety and depressive disorders were the most prevalent types. Due in large part to the COVID-19 epidemic, the number of individuals suffering from anxiety and depression illnesses increased dramatically in 2020. According to preliminary forecasts, anxiety and major depressive disorders would rise by 26% and 28%, respectively, in just a single year. Even while there are options for effective prevention and therapy, most people who suffer from mental problems lack access to quality care. In addition, a lot of people discrimination, stigma, and human rights violations.

BOOK ONE

ANXIETY DISORDER

A total of 301 million individuals, including 58 million children and adolescents, had an anxiety disorder in 2019. Excessive worry and fear, as well as associated behavioral abnormalities, are hallmarks of anxiety disorders. The severity of the symptoms is such that they cause substantial anguish or functional impairment. There are many distinct types of anxiety disorders, including separation anxiety disorder (which is characterized by excessive fear or anxiety about being apart from those with whom the person has a deep emotional bond), generalized anxiety disorder (which is characterized by excessive worry), panic disorder (which is characterized by panic attacks), social anxiety disorder (which is characterized by excessive fear and worry in social situations), and others. There is proven psychological treatment available, and medication may also be taken into consideration based on the patient's age and severity. Anxiety is a normal stress response. Mild anxiety might be advantageous in certain instances. It can warn us about threats and help us prepare and pay attention. Anxiety disorders differ from typical uneasiness or anxiousness in that they entail excessive fear or anxiety. Anxiety disorders are the most prevalent mental disorders. Almost 30% of adults experience them at some point throughout their lives. Anxiety disorders, on the other hand, can be treated using a variety of psychotherapy approaches. Treatment enables most people to live normal, productive lives.

Anxiety is defined as the expectation of a future issue and is often accompanied with muscle tension and avoidance behavior. Fear is an emotional reaction to an imminent threat that is more connected with a fight or flight response, which means staying to fight or fleeing to avoid danger. Anxiety disorders might cause people to avoid circumstances that cause or exacerbate their symptoms. Job performance, schooling, and personal relationships may be impacted. In general, a person can be diagnosed with an anxiety disorder if the fear or anxiety is out of proportion to the situation or age-inappropriate and reduce their ability to function normally. Anxiety symptoms can be physical, emotional, or behavioral, and may include:

Physical symptoms: increased heart rate, sweating, shaking, shortness of breath, dizziness, or gastrointestinal difficulties.

Emotional symptoms: fear, restlessness or irritation.

Behavioral symptoms: Avoidance of anxiety-inducing circumstances, difficulties concentrating, or compulsive behavior.

There are many types of Anxiety disorders discussed below;

- **Generalized Anxiety Disorder:** Generalized anxiety disorder is characterized by continuous and excessive worry that interferes with daily activities. This constant stress and tension may be accompanied by bodily symptoms such as restlessness, irritability or weariness, difficulty focusing, muscle tension, or difficulties sleeping. Worries are often about ordinary things like job commitments, family health, or little issues like chores, auto maintenance, or appointments.

- **Phobias (Specific phobia and Agoraphobia):** A specific phobia is an overwhelming and persistent fear of a particular object, place, or action that is not inherently harmful. Patients realize their fear is extreme, yet they are unable to overcome it. These anxieties cause so much distress that some people may go to tremendous lengths to escape them. Examples include a fear of public speaking, flying, and spiders. Agoraphobia is the fear of being in situations where escape is difficult or embarrassing, or where support is unavailable in the event of panic symptoms. The fear is out of proportion to the real circumstance, lasts for six months or longer, and impairs functioning. People who are agoraphobic express fear in any of the following; Using public transport, being in an enclosed or open space, being outside the home alone or standing in a queue. They actively avoid the situation, require a companion, or suffer from acute fear or anxiety. Without treatment, agoraphobia can progress to the point where a person is unable to leave their home. A person can only be diagnosed with agoraphobia if their fear is extremely unpleasant or significantly interferes with their daily activities.

- **Separation Anxiety Disorder:** A person suffering from separation anxiety disorder experiences extreme worry or anxiety over being separated from persons to whom he or she is attached. The feeling beyond what is appropriate for the person's age, lasts (at least four weeks in children and six months in adults), and impairs functioning. A person suffering from separation anxiety disorder may be continually concerned about losing the person dearest to him or her, be uncomfortable or unwilling to go out or sleep away from home or without that person, or have nightmares about separation. Physical symptoms of distress are commonly present in childhood, although they can persist into maturity.

- **Social Anxiety Disorder:** A person suffering from social anxiety disorder is extremely anxious and uncomfortable

about being embarrassed, humiliated,

rejected, or looked down upon in social

situations. People with this disorder will

either avoid or suffer the circumstance

with tremendous anxiety. Common

instances include intense dread of

public speaking, meeting new people,

and eating/drinking in public. The fear

or worry interferes with daily activities

and lasts at least six months.

- **Selective Mutism:** Children with

  selective mutism do not talk in certain

  social circumstances when they are

  expected to speak, such as school,

despite speaking in other situations. They will speak in front of closest family members at home, but rarely in front of outsiders, such as close friends or grandparents. Children with this illness may struggle with social communication due to a lack of speech, although they may also use nonverbal ways (e.g., grunting, pointing, writing). A lack of speech can also have serious effects at school, resulting in scholastic issues and social isolation. Many children with selective mutism exhibit excessive shyness, dread of social shame, and high levels of social anxiety.

However, they usually have normal

verbal skills.

CAUSES OF ANXIETY

The causes of anxiety disorders are currently unknown, however they are most likely caused by a mix of genetic, environmental, psychological, and developmental factors. Here is a detailed discussion of likely causes;

1. **Genetic factors (Hereditary and Genetic variations):** Anxiety problems typically run in families, indicating a genetic tendency. If a parent or close relative has an anxiety condition, it is more likely that

other family members may develop one. Certain genetic variations may impact brain chemistry and functioning, influencing how people respond to stress and regulate their emotions.

2. **Biological factors (Brain chemistry and Brain structure and function):** Dopamine, serotonin, and norepinephrine are important neurotransmitters that regulate mood and anxiety. Imbalances in these chemical substances may contribute to anxiety disorders.

Differences in brain areas such as the amygdala, which processes fear and threat reactions, and the hippocampus, which is involved in memory formation, can be associated with anxiety. Overactivity in these areas may predispose people to anxiety.

3. **Medical factors (Medications and Physical health conditions):** Anxiety is one of the possible negative effects of many drugs. Certain asthma treatments, steroids, and antidepressants, for example, have been shown to cause anxiety.

Certain medical illnesses, such as heart disease, diabetes, thyroid issues (such as hyperthyroidism), respiratory difficulties, and chronic pain, can cause or worsen anxiety feelings.

4. Developmental factors (Childhood experiences and Developmental stages):
Individuals who have insecure attachments and a lack of a supportive care-giving environment during their early childhood are more likely to experience anxiety. Different stages of development present unique stressors and obstacles that can impact the genesis of anxiety disorders. Adolescence is a pivotal period with major social and emotional development.

5. Environmental factors (Life circumstances, Trauma, Substance abuse):
Major life changes, such as moving,

changing jobs, or facing financial troubles,

can cause worry. Chronic stress from

ongoing challenges, such as employment

stress or relationship problems, might also

help.

Exposure to stressful or traumatic situations,

particularly in childhood, such as abuse,

neglect, or the death of a loved one, might

raise the chance of developing anxiety

disorders.

Using or withdrawing from some

substances, such as caffeine, alcohol,

narcotics, and certain prescriptions, can

cause anxiety symptoms.

Other causes include psychological factors, social factors, behavioral factors, and so on.

DIAGNOSE, TREATMENT AND SELF-HELP

Consider the follow steps while diagnosing anxiety disorders;

1. **Clinical Evaluation:** Anxiety disorder is often diagnosed via a thorough clinical interview conducted by a healthcare provider, which includes questions about the patient's medical history, present symptoms, and daily life impact. Clinicians frequently utilize standardized questionnaires and scales to assess the intensity of symptoms, such as the

Generalized Anxiety Disorder 7 (GAD-7),

Hamilton Anxiety Rating Scale (HAM-A), or

Beck Anxiety Inventory (BAI).

2. **Differential Diagnosis:** Anxiety

symptoms may coexist with other

psychiatric or physical problems. Clinicians

must distinguish anxiety disorders from

other illnesses such depression, PTSD,

thyroid issues, heart disease, and substance

misuse. A physical check and lab testing

may be required to rule out underlying

medical conditions that could be causing

anxiety symptoms.

3. Comprehensive Evaluation: A
comprehensive psychological assessment
may be performed to better understand
the patient's mental state, coping
techniques, and the presence of any co-
occurring mental health issues. Evaluating
how anxiety affects daily functioning, such
as employment, relationships, and social
interactions.

TREATMENTS OF ANXIETY DISORDERS

1. **Psychotherapy:** Cognitive Behavioral
Therapy(CBT) is a highly successful
treatment for anxiety disorders. It entails
recognizing and confronting problematic
thought patterns and behaviors, and then

replacing them with more adaptive ones. This therapy is especially beneficial for phobias and social anxiety because it gradually exposes patients to anxiety-provoking stimuli in a controlled manner, reducing sensitivity. Also, accepting anxiety as a normal part of life and commits to activities that are consistent with personal beliefs.

2. **Medications:** Commonly prescribed drugs include fluoxetine, sertraline, venlafaxine, duloxetine, alprazolam and diazepam. These are typically not recommended for long-term use due to

the risk of dependence. However, kindly
see a physician for guidance.

3. **Lifestyle and self-help activities:**
Regular physical activity can significantly
reduce anxiety symptoms. Maintaining a
balanced diet and avoiding caffeine and
alcohol can help manage anxiety.
Also,ensuring adequate and quality sleep is
crucial for mental health.

CURE FOR ANXIETY DISORDERS

1. Long term management involving
psychotherapy, particularly CBT, can help
maintain improvements and prevent

relapse (learning and practicing coping strategies to manage future stressors and triggers is essential).

2. Alternative therapies like Acupuncture and herbal remedies.

3. Social support groups, family and friends: Joining a strong support network can provide emotional support and encouragement.

4. Personalized treatment plans, where treatment plans should be individualized based on the patient's specific symptoms, preferences, and response to different therapies.

BOOK TWO

DEPRESSION (DEPRESSIVE DISORDER)

Depression is a complex mental health illness defined by a continuous and severe sense of melancholy or sadness, or a loss of interest in external stimuli. It influences how a person feels, thinks, and behaves, which can lead to a variety of emotional and physical issues. Depression differs from normal mood swings and changes about daily living. It can have an impact on every part of life, including connections with family, friends, and the community. It can result in or contribute to troubles at school and job. Depression can affect anyone. People who have experienced abuse, catastrophic losses, or other traumatic experiences are more likely to become depressed. Women are more likely to experience depression than men.

In 2019, 280 million individuals, including 23 million children and adolescents, suffered from depression. Mood swings and transient emotional reactions to day-to-day obstacles are not the same as depression. A depressive episode occurs when a person feels down for the most part of the day, almost every day, for at least two weeks. They may also experience a loss of pleasure or interest in activities. A number of additional symptoms may also be present, such as difficulty concentrating, feelings of extreme guilt or low self-worth, hopelessness regarding the future, suicidal thoughts, disturbed sleep, changes in eating or weight, and an unusually low level of energy or tiredness. Suicide is more common in those who feel depressed. However, effective psychological treatment may also be taken into consideration, depending on the age and severity of the condition.

Key Facts

- Depression is a frequent mental disease.

- About 5% of adults are depressed globally.

- Women are more likely than men to experience depression.

- Suicide is a possible outcome of depression.

- There are effective treatments for any level of depression.

POSSIBLE CAUSES OF DEPRESSION

Depression is the outcome of a complex interaction of social, psychological, and biological factors. People who have had negative life experiences (unemployment, bereavement, traumatic incidents) are more likely to develop depression. Depression can lead to increased stress and dysfunction, worsening both the affected person's life situation and the depression itself. Detailed causes are discussed below;

1. Biological factors (Genetics, Hormones, Brain chemistry): A family history of depression increases the risk. Hormonal changes caused by pregnancy, postpartum, thyroid issues, or menopause can all contribute to depression. Also, imbalances in neurotransmitters like dopamine, serotonin, and norepinephrine have been related to depression.

2. Environmental factors (Substance usage, Social isolation): Drug and alcohol misuse can both cause and exacerbate depression. Depression can be exacerbated by a lack of support networks and feelings of isolation.

3. Psychological factors (Trauma, Stress, Personality traits): Traumatic events, persistent stress, or significant life changes (such as the death of a loved one, relationship problems, or financial issues) can all cause depression. Also, people who have low self-esteem, are quickly overwhelmed by stress, or are typically gloomy are more likely to develop depression.

SYMPTOMS AND PATTERNS OF DEPRESSION

During a depressive episode, a person feels depressed (sad, irritated, empty). They may experience a lack of enjoyment or interest in certain activities. A depressive episode differs from normal mood changes. Depression can cause problems in every aspect of life, including the community, the household, the workplace, and school. Possible symptoms of depression are categorized into the following;

1. **Emotional symptoms:** A persistent sense of sadness, emptiness, or

hopelessness that lasts for the most of the day, almost every day. Loss of interest or pleasure in previously enjoyable activities, such as hobbies, social interactions, and sex. Excessive or inappropriate emotions of guilt or worthlessness, with frequent self-critical thoughts and rumination.

2. **Physical symptoms:** Insomnia or hypersomnia (too much sleep). An early morning awakening can also be an indication. Significant weight loss or increase while not dieting; appetite changes. Persistent fatigue and a lack of vitality, even after enough rest can also be noticed.

3. **Cognitive symptoms:** Difficulty focusing, making judgments, or remembering information. A widespread negative attitude about life, the future, and oneself. Struggling to make judgments, especially on relatively simple issues. Recurrent thoughts of death, or suicide attempts.

4. **Behavioral symptoms:** Avoidance of social situations and activities. Difficulty balancing duties at job, school, or home. Increased use of alcohol, drugs, or other substances to cope with depressive symptoms.

Depression can manifest in various patterns, with symptoms varying in intensity and duration. Here are some common patterns:

- Major Depressive Disorder (MDD)

- Seasonal Affective Disorder (SAD)

- Persistent Depressive Disorder (Dysthymia)

- Premenstrual Dysphoric Disorder (PMDD)

- Postpartum Depression

DIAGNOSIS AND TREATMENT

Depression can be effectively treated. These consist of psychological treatment, medications and counseling. If you have depressive symptoms, get help.

1. **Psychological treatments:** The primary line of treatment for depression is psychological. They can be used in conjunction with antidepressants for moderate to severe depression. Antidepressants are not required for mild depression. Psychological therapy can teach individuals new ways to think, cope, and interact with others. They may incorporate professional talk therapy as well as lay therapist supervision. Talk therapy can be conducted in person or online. Self-help manuals, websites, and apps provide access to psychological therapy.

2. **Clinical Interview:** The healthcare professional inquires about the patient's medical history, family history of mental health issues, personal history of mood disorders, substance use, and any recent significant life changes or stressors.

The clinician assesses the presence, duration, and severity of depressive symptoms, which may include chronic sadness, loss of interest or pleasure in activities, changes in appetite or weight, sleep disturbances, fatigue, feelings of worthlessness or excessive guilt, difficulty concentrating, and recurrent thoughts of death or suicide.

3. Use of Diagnostic Criteria like DSM-5 which provides specific criteria for diagnosing depressive disorders.

4. **Psychological Assessments:** Involves using self-report questionnaires are often used to quantify the severity of depression and monitor treatment progress.

Other effective treatment options include pharmacotherapy, pharmacotherapy, support system, self-care.

If you ever have thoughts of suicide:

- remember you are not alone and that many others have received help.

- reach out to someone you trust.

- consult a health worker, or join a support group.

If you believe you are in immediate risk of injuring yourself, call any available emergency services or a crisis line.

BOOK THREE

BIPOLAR DISORDER

Bipolar disorder (manic-depressive illness) is a mental disorder that produces unexpected fluctuations in a person's mood, energy, activity level, and concentration. These adjustments can make it difficult to do routine chores. These mood swings can disrupt sleep, energy levels, behavior, and cognitive function. Bipolar illness is a chronic condition, which means it will last a lifetime; however, with proper treatment, people can control their symptoms and live productive lives.

Over 40 million people worldwide suffered from bipolar illness in 2019. Bipolar disorder patients alternate between manic symptoms and depressed spells. When someone is going through a depressive episode, they usually feel down for the majority of the day, almost every day. They may also feel irritated, empty, or sad. In addition to euphoria or irritation, increased activity or energy, and other symptoms like talkativeness, racing thoughts, elevated self-esteem, decreased sleepiness, distractibility, and impulsive, risky conduct, manic symptoms can also include these. Bipolar disorder patients have a higher risk of suicide. However, there are successful therapy options, such as medication, stress reduction, and social functioning enhancement and psychoeducation. Changes in energy levels, sleep habits, capacity to focus, and other symptoms can have serious consequences for a person's behavior, career, relationships, and other parts of life. Most people experience mood swings at some point in their lives, but those caused by bipolar illness are more severe. Other symptoms may also occur. For example, some people with bipolar disorder suffer from psychosis, which might include: delusions, hallucinations, and paranoia.

Between episodes, a person's mood may be stable for months or years, especially if they are following a treatment plan.

TYPES OF BIPOLAR DISORDER

Bipolar I Disorder: This is defined by manic episodes lasting at least seven days or manic symptoms severe enough to require urgent hospital attention. Depressive episodes do occur, and they normally last at least two weeks. It is also possible to have episodes of depression with mixed features of depressive and manic symptoms occurring simultaneously.

Manic episodes are characterized by heightened, expansive, or irritated moods along with increased activity or energy. Symptoms include high self-esteem, a decreased desire for sleep, talkativeness, racing thoughts, distractibility, increased goal-directed activities, or dangerous behavior.

Bipolar II Disorder: This is defined by a pattern of depressive and hypomanic episodes rather than the full-blown manic episodes found in Bipolar I Disorder.

Hypomania is similar to mania, but less intense. Hypomanic episodes are less disruptive to daily life than manic episodes and last less time.

Cyclothymia: Cyclothymic Disorder: This is characterized by intervals of depressive and hypomanic symptoms that last for a minimum of two years (or one year in the case of children and adolescents), but not a depressive or hypomanic episode, according to the diagnostic criteria.

PHASES AND SYMPTOMS OF BIPOLAR DISORDER

Manic phase

- Euphoria: Elevated mood/excessive happiness, or sudden irritability.

- Talkativeness: Rapid speech, jumping from one topic to an unrelated one.

- Risky behavior: Engaging in activities that could have negative consequences, such as spending sprees, unprotected sex, or reckless driving.

- Grandiosity: Unrealistic beliefs in one's abilities.

Depressive phase

- Depressed mood: Feeling sad, hopeless, or empty.

- Fatigue: Decreased energy level.

- Cognitive impairments: Lack of concentration, inability to make decisions.

- Anhedonia: Loss of interest or pleasure in most activities, or isolation.

- Thoughts of death or suicide.

CAUSES OF BIPOLAR DISORDER

Generic factors: Bipolar disorder typically runs in families. Individuals with a family history of bipolar disorder are more prone to develop the illness.

Biological factors: People with bipolar disorder exhibit physical alterations in their brains. The importance of these changes is still unknown, although they may eventually assist determine causes.

Environmental factors: Stress, traumatic situations, and substantial life changes can all cause or exacerbate the disease.

Neurotransmitter Imbalance: An imbalance in neurotransmitters (chemicals in the brain) may be responsible for mood changes.

DIAGNOSIS AND TREATMENT

The diagnosis is based on self-reported experiences, behavior patterns, way of life observed by friends or family, and medical history. A thorough psychiatric evaluation is required, and sometimes a physical examination or laboratory tests are performed to rule out other causes. Treatments are not limited to the following;

- **Medications:** The use of Antidepressants along side mood stabilizers like Lithium, lamotrigine, valproate, carbamazepine. Also, Antipsychotics like olanzapine, aripiprazole, risperidone etc can be used.

- **Psychotherapy:** Here, Cognitive Behavioral Therapy (CBT) and Psychoeducation can be used to manage symptoms and educate victims of their families about the disorder.

- **Lifestyle and Self-care:** Through maintaining a consistent daily routine, adequate balanced dieting, regular physical exercises, and avoidance of substance usage.

- **Support system:** Connecting with others who suffer the same or related disorders can render support and advice, while also encouraging family and friend involvement can enhance treatment outcomes.

BOOK FOUR

POST-TRAUMATIC STRESS DISORDER

(PTSD)

In environments where there is conflict, there is a high prevalence of PTSD and other mental illnesses. After being exposed to a terrifying or very frightening event, or series of events, PTSD may develop. It embodies all of the following qualities:

- Re-experiencing the traumatic event or events in the present (intrusive memories, flashbacks, or nightmares).

- Ignoring thoughts and memories of the event or events.

- Staying away from people, places, or activities that bring back memories of the event or events.

- Persistently feeling as though there is a greater threat now.

These symptoms significantly hinder functioning and last for at least a few weeks. There are psychological treatments that work.

PTSD has been referred to by a variety of names in the past, including "shell shock" during World War I and "combat fatigue" following World War II, but it does not affect only combat veterans. PTSD affects people of all ethnicities, nationalities, and cultures, and at any age. Each year, around 3.5 percent of adults in the United States suffer from PTSD. The lifetime prevalence of PTSD in teenagers aged 13 to 18 is 8%. It is estimated that one in every eleven persons will be diagnosed with PTSD during their lifetime. Women are twice as likely as males to get PTSD. Three ethnic groups—U.S. Latinos, African Americans, and Native Americans/Alaska Natives—are disproportionately afflicted and have greater rates of PTSD than non-Latino whites. People with PTSD have powerful, unsettling thoughts and sensations about their experience that persist long after the traumatic incident has occurred. They may relive the event in flashbacks or dreams, experience sadness, dread, or fury, and feel disconnected or estranged from others. People with PTSD may avoid circumstances or people who remind them of the traumatic experience, and they may have significant negative emotions to something as ordinary as a loud noise or an unexpected touch.

SYMPTOMS OF PTSD

Generally, symptoms of PTSD fall into the following four broad categories. However, specific symptoms can vary in severity.

1. Intrusive Memories: Intrusive thoughts include recurring, involuntary memories; painful nightmares; and flashbacks to the traumatic occurrence. Flashbacks can be so vivid that people believe they are reliving the painful event or seeing it before their eyes.

2. Avoidance: To avoid reminders of the traumatic experience, avoid persons, places, activities, items, and situations that may elicit upsetting recollections. People may try not to remember or think about the traumatic experience. They may avoid discussing what happened or how they feel about it.

3. **Alterations in arousal and reactivity:** Arousal and reactive symptoms can include being irritated and having furious outbursts, behaving recklessly or in a self-destructive manner, being too suspicious of one's surroundings, being easily startled, or having difficulty concentrating or sleeping.

4. **Negative Changes in Thinking and Mood:** Inability to remember important aspects of the traumatic event, negative thoughts and feelings leading to ongoing and distorted beliefs about oneself or others (e.g., "I am bad," "No one can be

trusted"); distorted thoughts about the cause or consequences of the event leading to wrongly blaming self or others; ongoing fear, horror, anger, guilt, or shame, much less interest in previously enjoyed activities, feeling detached or estranged from others etc.

CAUSES OF PTSD

A wide range of distressing experiences might trigger PTSD. The specific cause is not entirely understood, although it involves a complex interaction of elements;

1. Traumatic Event Exposure:

- Childhood abuse: Physical, sexual, or emotional abuse during childhood significantly increases the risk.

- Serious accidents: Car accidents, plane crashes, or other life-threatening incidents can trigger PTSD.

- Sexual assault and domestic violence: Survivors of rape, sexual assault, and domestic violence are at high risk.

- Combat exposure: Veterans and military personnel often develop PTSD due to exposure to combat and life-threatening situations.

- Others are natural disasters (earthquakes, hurricanes) and sudden death of a loved one.

2. Biological factors:

- Genetics: A family history of anxiety and depression can cause PTSD.

- Neurotransmitter regulation: Irregularity of neurotransmitters, such as serotonin, can cause PTSD.

- Brain structure: Abnormalities in brain structure, such as abnormalities in the size of hippocampus, have been associated to post-traumatic stress disorder.

3. Environmental factors: Unavailability of strong support system and Continued exposure to stressors after the traumatic event may lead to PTSD.

4. Psychological factors:

- Pre-existing mental health conditions: Individuals with a history of depression, anxiety, or other mental health disorders are more vulnerable.

- Personality traits: Certain traits, such as high levels of neuroticism, can increase the likelihood of developing PTSD.

- Coping mechanisms: Ineffective coping strategies, such as substance abuse, can exacerbate symptoms.

Many people who have been exposed to a traumatic event suffer symptoms similar to those listed above in the days that follow the occurrence. To be diagnosed with PTSD, a person's symptoms must continue more than a month and produce severe distress or difficulty in their everyday functioning. Many people have symptoms within three months of the incident, although they might arise later and last for months or even years. PTSD is frequently associated with other linked conditions such as depression, substance abuse, memory impairments, and other physical and mental health issues.

Below provides a brief descriptions of four conditions related to PTSD.

Acute Stress Disorder: Acute stress disorder develops in response to a traumatic experience, just as PTSD, and the symptoms are identical. However, the symptoms appear between three days and a month following the occurrence. People with acute stress disorder may relive the event, experience flashbacks or dreams, and feel numb or distant from themselves. These symptoms cause significant distress and challenges in their daily lives. Around half of persons with acute stress disorder develop PTSD. Acute stress disorder has been diagnosed in 19%-50% of those who have experienced interpersonal violence (such as rape, assault, or intimate partner violence).

Adjustment Disorder: Adjustment disorder develops in reaction to a stressful life event (or events). The emotional or behavioral symptoms that a person experiences in response to a stressor are usually more severe or intense than what would be reasonably expected for the type of incident that occurred. Symptoms may include feeling stressed, unhappy, or hopeless; withdrawing from others; acting defiantly or impulsively; or experiencing bodily manifestations such as tremors, palpitations, and headaches. The symptoms create severe distress or difficulty functioning in important aspects of one's life, such as at job, school, or in social relationships. Symptoms of adjustment disorders appear within three months following a stressful event and continue no more than six months after the stressor or its consequences have passed. About 5% to 20% of people in outpatient mental health care have a primary diagnosis of adjustment disorders. A recent study discovered that more than 15% of persons with cancer experienced adjustment problem. It is usually treated with psychotherapy.

Disinhibited Social Engagement Disorder: This occurs in children who have suffered acute social neglect or deprivation prior to the age of two. Similar to reactive attachment disorder, it can develop when children lack the basic emotional needs for warmth, stimulation, and affection, or when frequent changes in caregivers (such as frequent foster care changes) prevent them from building solid relationships. Disinhibited social engagement disorder occurs when a youngster exhibits overly familiar or culturally inappropriate conduct with unknown adults. For example, the youngster may be willing to leave with an unfamiliar adult with little or no hesitation. Developmental difficulties, including cognitive and language disabilities, are frequently associated with this condition. Caregiving quality has been demonstrated to influence the progression of this condition. The incidence of disinhibited social interaction disorder is unknown, but it is believed to be uncommon. Most highly neglected youngsters do not develop the condition. The most crucial therapy modality is to collaborate with caregivers to provide the child with an emotionally available attachment figure.

Reactive Attachment Disorder: Occurs in children who have undergone extreme social neglect or deprivation in their early years of life. It can happen when children don't have the basic emotional needs for comfort, stimulation, and affection, or when they can't build stable bonds because of frequent caregiver changes. Children with reactive attachment disorder experience emotional withdrawal from their adult caregivers. They rarely seek comfort, assistance, or protection from caretakers, and they do not respond to consoling when disturbed. During typical encounters with caretakers, kids demonstrate little positive emotion and may exhibit unexplainable dread or melancholy. The difficulties appear before the age of five. Developmental difficulties, particularly cognitive and language disabilities, are frequently associated with the disease.

TREATMENT OF PTSD

It is pertinent to understand that not everyone who encounters trauma develops

PTSD, and not everyone who develops PTSD requires psychiatric therapy. For some people, PTSD symptoms fade or diminish over time. Others recover with the assistance of their support network (family or friends). Many persons with PTSD, however, require professional treatment to recover from profound and incapacitating psychological distress. It is crucial to realize that trauma can cause considerable distress. That distress is not the individual's fault, and PTSD may be treated. The earlier a person seeks treatment, the better their chances of recovery. However, possible treatments include but not limited to the following;

1. Therapies:

- Cognitive Behavioral Therapy (CBT): This focuses on changing negative thought patterns.

- Exposure Therapy: Involves safely exposing individuals to the trauma memories to help them overcome their fears.

- Group Therapy: This allows victims to share experiences and support each other on regular basis.

2. Medications:

- Antidepressants: Such as selective serotonin reuptake inhibitors (SSRIs) like sertraline (Zoloft) and paroxetine.

- Prazosin: Often used to treat nightmares related to PTSD.

- Anti-anxiety medications: Can help manage severe anxiety and related symptoms.

3. Self-care and lifestyle:

- Healthy diet: Can improve overall well-being.

- Mindfulness and relaxation routines: Such as yoga, meditation, and deep breathing exercises.

- Regular physical activity: Helps reduce stress and improve mood.

Avoiding alcohol and drugs: Substance usage should be completely stopped.

4. Support systems: Family, friends and strong support systems should provide emotional support and understanding.

BOOK FIVE

SCHIZOPHRENIA

Schizophrenia is a significant mental health illness that affects people's thoughts, feelings, and behaviors. It may cause a combination of hallucinations, delusions, and disorganized thought and behavior. Hallucinations are when you see or hear things that no one else can see. Delusions are strong convictions about things that aren't true. People with schizophrenia often appear to lose touch with reality, making daily life difficult. Approximately 24 million people, or 1 in 300 persons, globally suffer with schizophrenia. The life expectancy of people with schizophrenia is 10–20 years lower than that of the general population. Schizophrenia is characterized by notable behavioral abnormalities and perceptual deficits. Extreme agitation, disorganized thinking, hallucinations, persistent delusions, and severely disorganized conduct are some symptoms. Schizophrenia patients may have ongoing problems with their cognitive abilities. However, there are a number of efficient therapy choices available, such as psychoeducation, medicine, family interventions, and psychosocial rehabilitation.

People with schizophrenia require lifelong therapy. This includes medication, psychotherapy, and assistance in learning how to manage everyday life tasks. Many research studies have looked at the outcomes of untreated psychosis since many persons with schizophrenia are unaware of their mental health condition and may not believe they require treatment. People with untreated psychosis frequently have more severe symptoms, require more hospitalizations, have poorer cognitive and processing skills and social outcomes, suffer injuries, and die. On the other hand, early treatment frequently helps reduce symptoms before major complications develop, improving the long-term outlook.

SYMPTOMS OF SCHIZOPHRENIA

Schizophrenia causes a variety of difficulties with people's thoughts, feelings, and behaviors. Symptoms include;

1. Positive Symptoms:

- Hallucinations: These include seeing or hearing things that others do not notice. For those with schizophrenia, these phenomena appear to be genuine. Hallucinations can affect any of the senses, but hearing voices is the most common.

- Delusions: Strongly held false beliefs that are not grounded in reality. Common delusions include paranoid delusions (thinking one is being persecuted) and delusions of grandeur (feeling one possesses remarkable abilities or renown).

- Disorganized speech and thinking: Difficulty organizing thoughts, which results in incoherent speech and difficulty understanding communication. Rarely, communication may include stringing together unrelated words in an incomprehensible order. This is sometimes known as "word salad."

- Extreme Movement Disorders: Agitated body movements or catatonia (lack of movement or response).

2. **Negative Symptoms:** People with schizophrenia may be unable to perform in the same way they did before their disease. For example, they may not bathe, make eye contact, or express emotions. They may speak in a monotone voice and be unable to experience pleasure. They may also lose interest in daily tasks, socialize less, and struggle to plan ahead. It involves alogia (decreased speech output), anhedonia (inability to experience pleasure), and avolition (Lack of motivation to initiate activities).

3. **Cognitive Symptoms:** These include Difficulty with planning, organizing, and abstract thinking, difficulty focusing or paying attention and having issues with working memory, making it hard to use and remember information.

CAUSES OF SCHIZOPHRENIA

1. Genetic Factors:

- Family medical history: Schizophrenia tends to run in families, indicating a hereditary predisposition. If one parent has schizophrenia, the risk for their child increases to around 10%.

- Specific Genes: There is no single gene that causes schizophrenia. Instead, numerous genetic alterations may interact to increase risk. Several genes, including DISC1, NRG1, and COMT, have been identified as potential contributors to the development of schizophrenia.

2. Brain Structure and Function:

- Neurotransmitter Imbalance: Dysregulation of neurotransmitters, specifically dopamine, is crucial. Overactivity of dopamine in specific brain circuits is hypothesized to contribute to positive schizophrenia symptoms, whilst underactivity in other pathways may be connected to negative symptoms.

- Brain Structure: Individuals with schizophrenia have been found to have structural abnormalities such as enlarged ventricles, lower gray matter volume, and variations in numerous brain regions (for example, the prefrontal cortex and hippocampus).

- Neurodevelopmental Hypothesis: Abnormal brain development in utero or in early childhood may lead to the start of schizophrenia. This includes the aberrant migration of neurons in the brain.

3. Environmental factors:

- Prenatal Exposure: Exposure to viruses, malnutrition, or stressful events during pregnancy can increase the risk.

- Early Trauma: Early life stressors, such as abuse, neglect, or significant loss, may lead to schizophrenia.

- Substance Use: Drug use, especially throughout adolescence, might cause or worsen symptoms. Cannabis use, in particular, has been associated with an elevated risk of schizophrenia.

4. Psychosocial Factors:

- Stress: High levels of stress can trigger or worsen symptoms

- Socioeconomic Status: Living in urban environments, social isolation, and experiencing discrimination, economic hardship may cause schizophrenia.

TREATMENTS OF SCHIZOPHRENIA

1. **Medication:** Through the use of both typical and atypical antipsychotics to help manage symptoms.

2. **Psychotherapy:** Cognitive Behavioral Therapy (CBT), family therapy, and social skills mastery. They help patients manage symptoms by changing negative thought patterns, improve communication while also improving social interactions.

3. **Lifestyle and Self-care:** These include healthy diet, exercise, stress management techniques, and avoiding alcohol and drugs. Schizophrenia is a complicated mental health illness influenced by a variety of genetic, biochemical, environmental, and behavioral variables. Its treatment needs a multimodal strategy that includes medication, psychotherapy, social support, and lifestyle modifications. Individuals with schizophrenia benefit tremendously from early diagnosis and intensive, tailored treatment strategies.

BOOK SIX

EATING DISORDERS

Eating disorders are serious and complex mental health issues that have an impact on both emotional and physical well-being. People with eating disorders have an unhealthy relationship with food, their weight, or their looks. They can have serious physical and emotional implications and are frequently linked to complicated underlying psychological concerns, rather than just food.

In 2019, about 14 million individuals, including over 3 million children and teenagers, suffered from eating disorders.

Anorexia nervosa and bulimia nervosa are two examples of eating disorders that are characterized by aberrant eating patterns, obsession with food, and significant body image and weight issues. severe health risk or damage, severe distress, or significant functioning impairment are caused by the symptoms or behaviors. Anorexia nervosa is linked to early mortality via suicide or medical issues, and it typically manifests during adolescence or early adulthood. Bulimia nervosa sufferers have a markedly higher risk of substance abuse, suicide thoughts, and medical issues. There are effective treatment methods available, such as cognitive-based therapy and family-based treatment.

TYPES OF EATING DISORDERS

There are different types of eating disorders. Sadly, some people experience more than one type of eating disorder. They include;

1. Anorexia Nervosa: Extreme dietary restriction, severe anxiety of gaining weight, and a distorted body image are common characteristics. These individuals frequently see themselves as overweight, even when they are dangerously underweight. People with anorexia nervosa severely restrict their meals and calories, sometimes to the point of self-starvation.

2. Bulimia Nervosa: People with bulimia nervosa binge or consume enormous amounts of food in a short period of time. They may then force themselves to expel the calories by vomiting, using laxatives, or exercising excessively in order to rid their bodies of the food and calories.

3. **Binge Eating Disorder (BED):** Characterized by recurring episodes of eating huge amounts of food, typically quickly and to the point of pain. Unlike bulimia, binge eating episodes do not result in compensatory behaviors, which frequently lead to overweight or obesity.

However, after binge, they do not purge food or burn calories through exercise. Instead, they feel uncomfortably full and may experience feelings of humiliation, regret, guilt or melancholy.

CAUSES OF EATING DISORDERS

A combination of biological factors (genetics, hormones), environment, factors (trauma, low-self esteem) and social factors (peer pressure,media influence) can contribute to the development of eating disorders. When other aspects of their lives become difficult to manage, some persons suffering from eating disorders may resort to extreme measures to restrict their food consumption or food groupings. An fixation with food develops into an unhealthy way of dealing with uncomfortable emotions or sentiments. Thus, eating disorders are about finding healthy ways to manage your emotions rather than about food.

SYMPTOMS OF EATING DISORDER

Each type of eating disorder has its specific symptoms. Since eating disorders frequently resemble dieting, diagnosing one can be challenging. Alternatively, an individual grappling with an eating problem could be unwilling to communicate their eating issues. You might observe the following general changes if you or a loved one suffers from an eating disorder:

1. **Anorexia Nervosa:** Symptoms are extreme weight loss, preoccupation with food, dieting, and body size, refusal to eat certain foods or kinds of food, brittle hairs and nails, dry skin,excessive exercise.

2. **Bulimia Nervosa:** Symptoms include frequent episodes of binge eating,severe dehydration, swelling in the cheeks or jaw area, vomiting, exercise exercise, feeling out of control during binge episodes, purging, vomiting, fasting, or excessive exercise, stained teeth from stomach acid.

3. Binge Eating Disorder: Symptoms are eating large amounts of food in a short time, eating when not hungry, irregular weight, feeling guilty or disgusted after eating, eating alone.

TREATMENTS FOR EATING DISORDERS

Doctors and mental health experts identify eating disorders. Your primary care physician may assess your symptoms, conduct a physical examination, and prescribe blood tests. A mental health counselor, such as a psychologist or psychiatrist, does a psychological evaluation to discover more about your eating habits and beliefs.

1. Medical Care: Regular health check-ups are recommended to address the disorder's physical impacts and hospitalization in extreme cases to control malnutrition and stabilize the health.

2. **Psychotherapy:** Cognitive Behavioral Therapy (CBT)-Changes unhealthy beliefs and behaviors around eating and body image by combining CBT techniques with mindfulness strategies to manage emotions and behaviors.

3. **Medications:** Through the use of Antidepressants like selective serotonin reuptake inhibitors (SSRIs) to address underlying depression or anxiety and antipsychotics.

4. Support Groups: To provide a sense of community and shared experiences. Also, through the supports of family and friends. Eating disorders are complicated diseases that necessitate a varied approach to therapy. Early intervention, combined with medical, nutritional, and psychological support, can significantly improve outcomes. Awareness and awareness of the underlying causes, symptoms, and accessible treatments are critical for successful management and recovery.

CONCLUSION

A mental disorder is defined as a clinically significant impairment in a person's cognition, emotional regulation, or behavior. It is typically associated with distress or impairment in key areas of functioning. There are numerous sorts of mental disorders. Mental disorders can also be known as mental health issues.

Mental health difficulties refer to a wide range of illnesses that influence emotion, thinking, and behavior. They can affect anyone, regardless of age, gender, or background, and the intensity ranges from moderate to severe. Examples are not limited to the following Anxiety disorders, Depressive disorders, Bipolar disorders, Post-Traumatic Stress Disorder (PTSD), Schizophrenia, Eating disorders etc.

Symptoms of mental health issues vary widely and include but not limited to persistent sadness or depression, confused thinking or reduced ability to concentrate, extreme mood swings, delusions, hallucinations, inability to cope with daily problems. Others are excessive fears, low energy, withdrawal from people, problems relating to people, substance abuse etc.

Causes could be biological (genes and hormones), environmental (past experiences, peer pressure), psychological (low self-esteem), social-cultural (media influence) etc.

Treatments and cure can be achieved through medications (antidepressants, anti-psychotics) regular medical care and monitoring, nutritional counselling, psychotherapy (CBT, IPT), support systems, and family and friends. Mental health is a crucial aspect of overall well-being, and addressing issues early can lead to better outcomes and improved quality of life.

WHO RESPONSE

The World Health Organization's Comprehensive Mental Health Action Plan 2013–2030 acknowledges the critical role mental health plays in promoting universal health. The strategy has four main goals:

- to improve mental health governance and effective leadership;

- to offer community-based mental health and social care services that are thorough, responsive, and integrated;

- to put into practice mental health promotion and preventive initiatives;

- to improve mental health research, evidence, and information systems.

Through the use of evidence-based technical guidelines, tools, and training materials, the WHO's Mental Health Gap Action Programme (mhGAP) aims to close the service gap in nations, particularly those with limited resources.